make things
HAPPEN

The Key to
Networking for Teens

by Lara Zielin

Lobster Press ™

Published by Lobster Press™
1620 Sherbrooke Street West, Suites C & D
Montréal, Québec H3H 1C9
Tel. (514) 904-1100 • Fax (514) 904-1101 • www.lobsterpress.com

Publisher: Alison Fripp
Editor: Julie Mahfood
Graphic Design & Production: Tammy Desnoyers

Distributed in the United States by:
Publishers Group West
1700 Fourth Street
Berkeley, CA 94710

Distributed in Canada by:
Raincoast Books
9050 Shaughnessey Street
Vancouver, BC V6P 6E5

We acknowledge the financial support of the Government of Canada through the Book Publishing Industry Development Program (BPIDP) for our publishing activities.

The Canada Council | Le Conseil des Arts
for the Arts | du Canada

We acknowledge the support of the Canada Council for the Arts for our publishing program.

National Library of Canada Cataloguing in Publication

Zielin, Lara, 1975-
    Make things happen: the key to networking for teens / Lara Zielin.

ISBN 1-894222-43-1

    1. Teenagers--Social networks--Juvenile literature.
2. Interpersonal relations in adolescence--Juvenile literature.
I. Title.

HQ796.Z53 2003   j302.2'24'0835   C2002-903916-9

Printed and bound in China.

To my best friend and husband, Justin, whose support and unconditional encouragement made this book possible.

ACKNOWLEDGEMENTS

I would like to thank the following people who selflessly gave their time, attention and information for Make Things Happen.

Julie Mahfood – an amazing editor and a pleasure to work with, Leah Haugen, Paulette Selvig, Angela Spence, Sheldon Hunt, Prasantha Jayakody, Esther Shin, Mark Teodoro, Erik Karulf, Dianne Myers, Rebecca Greene, Charles and Susan Zielin, Jimmy and Judy Magouirk, Christine Johnson D'Amico, Mary Lu Jackson, Jim and Stephanie Umberger, Anthony Beard, Kirsten King, and The Carleton College Career Center.

TABLE OF CONTENTS

SOME THINGS YOU'LL SEE IN THIS BOOK...

make things HAPPEN

is a book designed to take you on a networking journey. But every journey – no matter how short – should begin with a map.

The map for *Make Things Happen* looks something like this:

CHAPTER SECTIONS

Every chapter is broken up into sections to help you better digest the book's information. Chapter sections outline the big points the chapter is trying to make. Chapter section headings are always in **BOLD** print.

Subheadings

Lots of times there are smaller ideas within each chapter section. These ideas relate directly to the chapter sections, but they aren't big enough to stand on their own. These are called subheadings, and they're noted in *italics*.

Along the way, you'll see some asides and comments scattered throughout the pages. These are information supplements – or networking vitamins – and they come in different shapes and sizes.

Keep your eyes peeled for the following:

CASE IN POINT

Case in Point boxes include real-life stories about people who network. These stories come from all over North America. They feature young men and women who have found a way to make networking work in their lives.

AIN'T IT A FACT

When you see the Ain't it a Fact box, you'll see an important fact or idea from the chapter you're reading.

Reminder Balloon

Reminder Balloons are for those of us who can't remember everything at once. Reminder Balloons will let you know there's something from another chapter that's being covered again.

Piece it Together

Piece it Together explains two related terms in more detail. The terms in the *Piece it Together* section can always be found in the glossary, too.

PICKING THE EXPERT'S BRAIN

No one resource can supply all the information you need, or want, to know. *Picking the Expert's Brain* lists books, Web sites and organizations where you can find out more about topics discussed in the chapter.

* When checking out the Web sites in this book, whether in the *Picking the Expert's Brain* section or otherwise, please remember that the World Wide Web is a growing, changing entity. The Internet addresses listed in this book have been checked for accuracy, but they are subject to change.

CHAPTER HIGHLIGHTS

- Chapter Highlights are just that – the chapter highlights! They review the major points covered in each chapter.

A *Glossary* is also found at the back of this book.

The *glossary* includes definitions of some important terms in the book. The list of words given in the *glossary* is in alphabetical order. When you run across a networking word you don't know, turn to the *glossary* for more information.

Now that you know what to expect from the chapters in this book, you can get to it! Have fun, and enjoy the journey!

CHAPTER 1. What Is Networking?

PERHAPS you've heard the expression that there are three types of people in the world: those who make things happen, those who watch things happen, and those who wondered what happened at all. The people in life who network successfully fall only into the first category of people: Those who *make* things happen.

The fact that you've picked up this book at all means you're already moving into the first category. Kudos and congratulations! But don't let your endeavors stop there. By following the principles outlined in this book, you can use networking to help you achieve your lifelong ambitions, in addition to achieving the goals you have in front of you right now.

"Begin doing what you want to do now. We are not living in eternity. We have only this moment, sparkling like a star in our hand – and melting like a snowflake."
– Marie Beynon Ray

RENEW YOUR MIND

For those of you already experiencing the mindset it takes to network, this book will provide further material to help you along the way; but if networking is new to you, then you should know that to use it properly, a paradigm shift in thinking must occur.

A paradigm is defined as a model, or an example. It can also be defined as a common way of thinking about a particular subject. A paradigm shift occurs when the old ways of thinking about and doing things are radically changed, and a whole new perspective is formed. To begin your own networking paradigm shift, it's important to understand that the networking journey involves strategic thinking concerning your life's path. Networking isn't just about meeting people. It's about meeting people who can help you make informed decisions about your life experience on this earth.

Every single one of us is influenced by someone or something, for better or for worse. Right now you can make a difference in your life by determining who you want to be influenced by. Make the decision to find people around you who can help you reach your life's goals. Find people who can help you answer important questions like "What do I want to do when I get out of school?" or "How can I obtain my current goals?"

The paradigm shift occurs when you begin, *right now*, to make decisions about where you think you might want to be in two weeks or in two years. The paradigm shift takes complete effect when you've launched yourself, 100%, into the category of someone *who makes things happen*.

Those who make things happen through networking can be further subdivided into two categories:

► The first group knows a little about networking, but most of their information is incorrect. Their knowledge is based on stereotypes gathered from TV, movies and other popular media outlets.

► The second group has knowledge about networking, and they use it as a tool. However, they do not use networking properly. This group thinks of networking simply as rubbing elbows with the right people to get what they want.

By the time you are finished with this book, you will not fall into either of the above categories. Rather, you will belong to a third group of networkers.

➤ The third group of networkers has accurate knowledge pertaining to networking's definition and purpose. This group puts their networking knowledge into practice by connecting with people around them in relationships that are genuine and mutually beneficial. For this group, networking is not a one-time incident, but rather a lifelong endeavor.

WHAT IS NETWORKING?

The networking process starts with the reader's sincere desire to discover more about the world around them, and more about themselves. When a person networks, they essentially seek out others for information and help, usually (though not always) in the area of career or work guidance. Depending on the networker's approach, the information givers may be strangers or friends.

Networking is a tool for those who want to better put their gifts and talents to work. Through networking, many find a means of doing things that might normally seem impossible.

Networking is part of a bigger, strategic career picture that involves thinking about the kinds of things you might enjoy doing in life, long before financial pressures force you to choose a vocation. You can be ahead of the game, thinking about your future now — *before* the clock starts ticking!

Maybe you're still wondering, "Why should I network?" After all, you might have a part-time job, after school and on weekends, which you like just fine. Maybe you're not even old enough to work yet. Chapter 2 will help answer some of these tough questions, since it explains, in detail, the importance of networking. But the challenge to you *now* is to begin thinking about what you were placed on this earth to accomplish — and begin taking steps toward that goal. Do something related to what you are passionate about! And don't worry if you don't yet know what that is. Chapters 3 and 4 will help you articulate your gifts, talents and dreams.

Unfortunately, many people never understand networking for what it is: a process of uncovering more about themselves and their careers. Some may look at networking as an unnecessary step in an already long path, asking, "Why network when the want ads say everything there is to say about a company's available positions?" The truth is that the want ads don't say everything there is to know about a job. In fact, the want ads can be downright misleading about some positions. In addition, the odds that you'll actually get a job by applying through the want ads are slim, as these ads represent only about 20% of available jobs on the market. Overall, networking goes much deeper than just finding a job.

Through networking you may:

▶ Uncover information to map out your goals and life plans

▶ Get advice and information from leaders and mentors

▶ Obtain well-rounded information about a company or companies

▶ Make connections that can lead to career opportunities

Best of all, networking doesn't have to be stuffy or contrived. It can be informal, which means you can chat with your Aunt Sue about her job and that is still considered networking. When you ask your neighbor to recommend a good pet-sitter, that's networking, too!

This book highlights the importance of informal networking within a structured setting. A structured setting means the networker has taken time to research who in their life might be a good networking contact, and why. Before the networker actually contacts that person, they've already outlined the purpose for the meeting or conversation, and know what they want to talk about. This type of networking takes time, forethought and energy, but the rewards are well worth the effort.

Angela Spence lives in Minneapolis, Minnesota, and is passionate about fine arts. Her interests include dancing, acting, modeling and theater.

Angela wants to begin developing her fine arts interest, but isn't sure exactly how to do that. At the very least, she knows she needs to learn about the industry and begin meeting people. To get the ball rolling, she responds to a commercial on television, advertising for extras in the Tim Allen movie Joe Somebody. A few days later, Angela is cast as an extra in the film, and begins a full-day shoot in downtown Minneapolis.

Between takes, Angela begins chatting with Tracy, the woman seated next to her. Angela soon learns that Tracy works for a casting company. Tracy, in turn, asks about Angela's interest in fine arts, and suggests Angela might want to do an internship at the casting company *where Tracy works. An internship would be a good way for Angela to learn about the business and make valuable connections. Intrigued, Angela decides to get more information and pursue this lead.*

Angela's story is a great example of networking. Ironically, if you asked Angela, she probably wouldn't even know she *was* networking! This type of networking falls neatly under the definition of informal networking, which will be covered in detail later in this chapter.

Like Angela, you may have an interest in something, but maybe you're not quite sure what to do next. Angela took a good first step simply by pursuing activities that were a fit with her skill-set. Angela doesn't want to be an extra in movies all her life, but she realized she could use the experience as a steppingstone to something else. And look what happened!

Angela's use of networking had some exciting results. Not only did she meet Tracy, a valuable contact, but she also learned of a potential internship opportunity. If Angela wants to further investigate the casting company – and the internship – she can meet with Tracy on more formal ground in what's called an informational interview or job shadow. Informational interviews and job shadows are more structured ways to network and acquire information. Both concepts will be discussed in detail in chapter 6, as will internships.

It is in Angela's best interest to learn as much as she can about the internship Tracy mentioned. Internships are great opportunities, but they can be demanding. Unlike informational interviews or job shadows, internships are sometimes paid. They also require scheduled attendance.

Job shadows, informational interviews and internships would all have the same ideal result for Angela: to teach her more about the world of fine arts, and help her evaluate where her skills and interests fit best within that world.

Angela has begun a networking journey in which one connection leads to another, then to another. That's why a network is defined as a series of connected things! Networking builds a web of contacts within the networker's sphere. These connections crisscross, weave and are dependent upon one another for stability. As long as Angela continues to build upon these relationships, she can call on them to uncover opportunities of interest.

WHAT NETWORKING IS *NOT*

How many movies have you seen where high-powered executives are talking to one another using lines like "Let's make a deal" and "I'll have my people call your people"? This stereotype is played out very strongly in the popular media. So strongly, in fact, that many think this is the correct way to go about networking. As a result, networking is often used as a means to achieve goals, while giving no thought to the other people involved.

When done incorrectly, networking can be an exhausting, unfulfilling experience. Imagine yourself constantly in the position of a person who needs something and will do nearly anything to get it. In this way, a bad networker becomes a chameleon, changing with each environment. Not only is it tiring to constantly change with circumstances, it's also wearying to try to fit the mold of what others expect, especially when you're not qualified to meet those expectations.

DIRECT CONTACT

Networking, as we've said, is building relationships to discover more about the world around you, especially as it relates to careers and jobs. Direct contact is a form of networking, but with a twist. Direct contact means networking solely for one purpose: employment. It means seeking out the people who do the hiring, and asking for a job.

AIN'T IT A FACT

Networking is much like a spider weaving a web. It's not the quantity of strands that's important, but the *quality* of the strands. Each one overlaps and interconnects with the other, creating a cohesive net.

Direct contact can be a great means to an end if what you want is a job. Many seasoned professionals network this way when changing employment fields.

If you choose to use direct-contact networking, keep in mind that all forms of networking involve sharing information, *not* exploiting people to get what you want. Honesty, genuine interest and respect must accompany each type of networking.

QUALITY, NOT QUANTITY

Networking does not mean meeting as many people as possible to add to a long list of friends. Rather, networking means seeking out specific people with specific information who can help you reach your goals. Networking is about quality more than quantity. Using the web analogy, it's not how many strands the web has which make it stable – it's the strength of the individual strands.

TYPEF OF NETWORKING

There are two types of networking being discussed in this book: targeted and informal[1]. We will concentrate primarily on informal networking. However, both types of networking are closely linked and the definitions can overlap. Therefore, it's important for us to understand each type.

Targeted Networking

Targeted networking is used primarily to find a job, or when changing careers. Targeted networking is used when a networker's career goals are laid out clearly and they know exactly what they want. Networkers then use targeted networking to find the people who can help them reach their end goal, which is usually an employment position. Like direct contact, targeted networking takes place within a narrow window of interest. Since the goal is fixed, the networker does not pursue a wide range of resources.

Informal Networking

Informal networking is networking that never stops. It is continuous and occurs in a variety of settings, with the primary motive being to build reciprocal relationships. Remember Angela's story and how she hardly even knew she was networking? That's exactly the kind of networking that informal networking is. It's so subtle and natural that the networker hardly even realizes it's going on!

Informal networking is the type of networking this book discusses the most. It is the perfect type of networking for those who are just starting to determine their goals in life.

---

[1] Kohen, Deb and Lee, Tony. *Career Choice, Change & Challenge: 125 Strategies from the Experts at careerjournal.com.* Indianapolis: Jist Works, 2000.

ENJOY THE JOURNEY

The idea behind informal networking is that it's used to gather information about occupations and businesses to help you better understand yourself and the kinds of things you would enjoy doing in life. So don't worry – you don't have to figure out exactly what you want to do or be in order to network successfully. In fact, sometimes it's better to network when you don't have those things figured out. In essence, networking is a tool to help you meet the people who can assist you in your journey of discovering what you were put on this earth to do.

CHAPTER HIGHLIGHTS

- Definition: According to author Joyce Lain Kennedy, "Networking means seeking out acquaintances, advice givers and potential friends, and systematically building on these relationships."[2]

- Networking is *not* seeking out others and using them to solely advance oneself.

- Successful networking is like weaving a web of contacts. The web should provide a strong support base for the networker.

- There are two types of networking: targeted and informal. Targeted networking is a narrower, more defined way of networking. Informal networking is a learning process which involves a wider variety of people.

---

[2] Kennedy, Joyce Lain and Laramore, Darryl, Ph.D. *Joyce Lain Kennedy's Career Book*. Lincolnwood: VGM Career Horizons, 1998.

PICKING THE EXPERT'S BRAIN

Here are some resources to help you learn more:

Bolles, Richard Nelson. *What Color is your Parachute?* **Berkeley: Ten Speed Press, 2002.**

Parachute is about discovering yourself in the process of discovering what you want to do in life. This book contains useful information on networking.

www.nextstepmagazine.com

This e-zine features articles for teen readers, and deals with subjects related to networking: careers, life paths, college preparation and more.

CHAPTER 2. Why Network?

NOW that you know what networking is, it's time to apply it to your life. But first you must understand one key factor: you *(yes, you!)* have immense value and worth as an individual on this planet. It's true! Think for a moment about the kinds of things that you love to do. Within that list of things – somewhere – there's something that you were put on this earth to accomplish. Your life is not a series of random coincidences, but rather it's purposeful and unique. Think about it: you are the only you on this planet. For that reason, there's something that you, and no one else, can offer the world. That's exciting! Networking is one way for you to begin to figure out what it is that you would like to contribute and accomplish in life.

"For the sake of making a living, we forget to live." – Margaret Fuller

Let's examine the four main reasons to network, which are to:

1. **Learn more about yourself**
2. **Plan ahead for the future**
3. **Get inside information about jobs or companies**
4. **Get expert/professional help or advice on a variety of topics**

Piece it Together ←

An occupation is an individual's job or profession.

An expert is one who is knowledgeable or skillful in a specific area.

LEARN MORE ABOUT YOURSELF

Networking is a great way for you to learn more about yourself. As you discuss your interests and goals with career professionals, you'll learn which jobs interest you and which don't. You'll start to visualize the type of environment where you see yourself succeeding. You will also find answers to questions like these:

▶ Would I prefer to wear a suit to work, or does a more casual environment appeal to me?

▶ Do I see myself working behind a desk, or out in the open?

▶ How much money do professionals in my area(s) of interest make?

▶ How much money do I want to make?

▶ What levels of experience and education will I need?

As you build relationships, you'll also build upon the information you already have about yourself. For example, if you love cars, do you see yourself working in an auto shop or in a car museum? If you love art, do you see yourself designing advertisements or working in an art gallery? Networking means thinking about your gifts and talents and how you will apply them in life.

PLANNING AHEAD

Chances are you'll have one or two letdowns in life. Maybe you've already experienced disappointments you weren't able to control. A divorce within the family, a death, a hard breakup with someone you really liked or loved – the list goes on. Some disappointments are out of our control and we must face them as a part of life. But other potential disappointments can be avoided by planning ahead.

One of the biggest disappointments that men and women all over the world experience is in their career path. Sadly, most people don't enjoy what they do in life. One out of every three people in the workplace today performs their job solely for the income it generates, enjoying little apart from the paycheck they get at the end of the week. Most people who find themselves in jobs they dislike are there because of a failure to plan. Planning for the future means taking steps to make sure it turns out the way you want it to. Networking can and should be a big part of planning for the future.

CASE IN POINT

Can you imagine how sad it would be to graduate from college and have no idea what kind of job you might like? Unfortunately, after studying for four years at one of the best colleges in the United States, I found myself in that exact situation.

In the spring of my senior year of college, I had no clue about how to use my degree in the real world. I had majored in anthropology at a liberal arts school, and didn't know what to do with my knowledge. Sadly, I wasn't sure there was anything I could do with it, so I decided to pursue a job doing something completely unrelated. I took a position at a high-tech company that paid well, and I thought I could be happy. I was wrong. I wasn't doing activities that I enjoyed or which gave me fulfillment; I ended up quitting. After that, I didn't do the research to determine what kind of job I might really like, so a month later I found myself in a different company doing more work that I hated.

I wasted three long years before I finally woke up and realized I had to start assessing my gifts, my goals and my priorities to start making things happen the way I wanted them to. I had to start networking to find people who were out in the real world achieving goals similar to the ones in my own heart.

Imagine if I had begun thinking strategically about career paths when I was in high school or in my early years of college! Imagine if, at the same time, I had begun networking and exploring careers that were interesting to *me*. I could have saved three years of misery and disappointment in my life. Don't make the same mistakes I did and wait until the last minute to begin networking and planning your career path.

Begin now to connect with people you know, and start a discussion about your goals for the future. Talk to people employed in jobs that you think you will want, in one, five, ten or fifty years. Learn what mistakes they made and what they wish they could change, and be wise enough to avoid the same pitfalls. Follow their formula for success, and then watch as your life does the same!

THE INSIDE SCOOP

Think about your favorite ice cream. Think about how it tastes. Now think of how you would describe that taste to a friend. Perhaps if your favorite flavor is mint-chocolate-chip, you might say, "The mint flavor in this ice cream is light and refreshing. It is accented by the rich, sweet flavor of the chocolate chips." Now think how much easier it would be for your friend to know the flavor of mint-chocolate-chip ice cream simply by tasting it. Experiencing the ice cream itself would open up a whole new world of flavor. The same is true of networking. There is only so much information about a profession that you can get from books, videos and the Internet. The real way to find out what a career is truly like is to talk to someone who performs that career on a day-to-day basis. Visiting their office and experiencing the environment will reveal a truer picture than books ever could.

Have you ever read an employment ad that asked for a "self starter"? How about one that demanded that the applicant "must be able to multi-task"? Ever wondered what those job descriptions mean? Many times, employment ads are vague at best, and sometimes they can even be misleading. Networkers often have the advantage of knowing what a position is really like *before* they apply. In fact, most networkers avoid the employment ads entirely. By connecting with people on the inside of an organization, they meet those who actually *do* the hiring. Networkers have beneficial face-to-face connections within the company before they ever submit a résumé. Here's a fact to keep in mind: on average, when you use the want ads as a means to apply for a job, your résumé has only *a 1 in 300 chance* of leading to an interview.

AIN'T IT A FACT

Networkers usually don't have to use the employment ads for job hunting. Many times, they have a face-to-face connection within a company before they ever submit a résumé.

NEED HELP?

Networking is a wonderful way to get expert opinions and advice. For example, if you know someone within an industry or profession which you'd like to explore, that person can offer you information you might not otherwise get, such as important résumé advice. Many times he or she can explain to you exactly how the employer likes to see résumés completed, what skills they like to see highlighted, and whether or not your résumé should come with references.

When you weave your web of contacts, you will try to learn which person can help you the most. When you learn who that key person is, use your contacts to also learn *about* that person. Do they prefer to meet people during the lunch hour or during business hours? Do they take phone calls at a certain time of day? (If so, make an appointment with them during that time only!) Do they like certain sports, or have particular affiliations? Knowing these things sure can make small talk a lot easier! There is an expression that says you are never more than a few people away from the person who holds the key to helping you make your dreams come true. If you are lucky enough to meet that person, don't miss your opportunity to really connect with them just because of a lack of information.

Networkers can also help you get hooked up with organizations that can teach and train you in specific areas. For example, I learned through networking that my home city, Minneapolis, has a number of organizations to help writers just like me. There are writing societies to meet other writers, and some that are geared just to help writers find jobs. There is a center for writing that provides classes and lectures. Networking helped me locate each of these resources and, once there, I usually had a contact to go to for additional help.

TRUE FULFILLMENT

At the core of its definition and purpose, networking exists to help you help yourself. Devoting your life to uncovering – then doing! – what you're good at, is a key to your happiness, success and fulfillment. Leaving your skills and passions undiscovered and unexplored is a great loss – both to you and the world around you. Think of what would have happened if Einstein had never explored physics! We might have lost one of the greatest minds to ever think about space and time. What if Michelangelo had never tried his hand at stone cutting? We might never have looked upon the sculptures of one of the greatest artists that ever lived. Taking steps to uncover areas where you can excel is really worthwhile. Keep in mind you might also have *transferable skills*, which means that your gifts and talents can be used in different settings. For example, if you have a love of animals and the outdoors, you might make a great veterinarian, park ranger or even a zoologist. There may be more than one career that is a good fit for you. In life, explore and do the things that come to you naturally. They're most likely easiest for you, and, chances are, that's what you're good at.

Think about how many times you've been asked, "What are you going to be when you grow up?" Usually people rack their brains trying to think of an occupation they could do for 40 hours a week and still find satisfaction. But stop for a moment to consider: the answer might not be in a job title. The answer to the question, "What are you going to be?" could simply be: *happy*. The response *should* be, "I want to be happy and fulfilled. I *don't* want to end up in a job I hate, doing work I don't enjoy. I *don't* want to get to the end of my life and have regrets." In your life, don't make a living just to make a living – don't do a job just to do a job. Find what you love and do it because it's an extension of you. Treat your life as a journey and figure out where you want to go. Then start!

CHAPTER HIGHLIGHTS

- The gifts and talents you possess can be used in a variety of professional settings.
- Network to discover which environments best suit you.
- Network in order to:
  1. Learn more about yourself
  2. Plan for the future
  3. Get the inside scoop on certain professions
  4. Get professional help and advice
- Don't ever do a job just to do a job. Do what you love because it's an extension of you and because you're passionate about it.

PICKING THE EXPERT'S BRAIN

Here are some resources to help you learn more:

Graham, Stedman. *Teens Can Make It Happen: Nine Steps to Success.* New York: Simon & Schuster, 2000.

Networking is one piece of a much bigger pie; author Stedman Graham helps teens make possibilities for success a reality.

McGraw, Jay. *Life Strategies for Teens.* New York: Fireside Publishing, 2000.

"Steer, don't drift" is the motto of this book. Author Jay McGraw helps teens take control of their lives at every turn.

www.tfs.net/~gbyron/main.html

This Web site, *Teen Guide to Making Money*, focuses on helping young people plan for financial success, and includes information about determining what you want from life and how to get it.

CHAPTER 3. Know Thyself!

NETWORKING is as much about knowing yourself as it is about knowing others. Before you begin meeting new people, take a moment to get to know yourself a little better. It's important to take an inventory of your skills, interests and dreams and then apply them to the networking process. You must ask yourself what kinds of experiences you want to have when you network and what kind of people you want to meet – in essence, what a fulfilling networking encounter would be like for you.

"Know thyself." – The Seven Sages

GETTING PERSONAL

Many of you reading this book may not, as yet, have well-defined interests. You might not know your own likes and dislikes enough to help focus your networking experiences. That's precisely the reason for this chapter, which is devoted to helping you uncover more information about the kinds of things that you like. You can then use what you've learned about yourself to network more effectively. For those of you who are ready to skip this chapter because you think you already know yourself pretty well, hold on a minute. You will change more than you expect in your lifetime. Sorting out who you are – your interests, skills and goals – is a lifelong journey. So chances are you don't know *everything* about yourself yet. The results of the exercises in this chapter just might surprise you.

Note: The following exercises are based loosely on the RIASEC model of occupations, which is the copyrighted work of Dr. John L. Holland and his publisher, Psychological Assessment Resources, Inc.

EXERCISE 1 - YOUR INTERESTS AND SKILLS

The following is designed to help you learn more about your interests and skills. Please complete the sentences below. Be as specific as possible. If there is an "(I)" next to the sentence, it means you're describing an interest. If there is an "(S)" next to the sentence, it means you're describing a skill.

➤ (S): I'm good at

➤ (S): A time I was successful was when

➤ (S): A time I was helpful was when

➤ (S): I have received compliments about

➤ (I): I really enjoy activities like

➤ (I): I'm happiest when I'm

➤ (I): My favorite subject in school is

➤ (I): If I could do anything I would

Piece it Together

An interest is a curiosity, focus, hobby or concern.

A skill is an aptitude or expertise.

Go back to your answers and study them for a moment. Do your answers have things in common? For example, if athletics and the outdoors were featured in your answers, then you probably enjoy being active. Note the difference between the skills you *have*, and the skills you *want*. If there are skills you want, you can use networking as a way to get them. For example, if you really want computer programming as a skill, talk to computer programmers. Find out how they got started, what kind of environments they work in and what they would recommend for someone in your position. In the same way, if there are skills that you already have but want to develop further, use networking to meet people who can help you.

EXERCISE II - YOUR BEST ENVIRONMENT

Examine the following chart to find out which environments may be best for you to network in.

QUESTION	ANSWER	ENVIRONMENT
Do you like to be around people? Is it important for you to have lots of friends?	If <u>yes</u>, then you might enjoy:	An environment full of people to interact with. <u>Networking Possibilities:</u> Radio or TV Stations, Talent Agencies, Salespersons, Public Relations
Do you like to work or play with different things? (e.g., wood, paint, makeup, animals, etc.) Do you like to be outside?	If <u>yes</u>, then you might enjoy:	An environment with many different mediums to work with. <u>Networking Possibilities:</u> Visual Artists, Sculptors, Hair Stylists, Photographers, Landscapers/Greenhouse Gardeners

QUESTION	ANSWER	ENVIRONMENT
Do you like numbers and data? Do you like to solve mysteries? Do you follow instructions well? Are you organized?	If yes, then you might enjoy:	An environment working with data or information. Networking Possibilities: High-tech Companies, Accountants, Professors or Teachers, Lawyers
Do you use your imagination a lot? Are you persuasive? Are you influential?	If yes, then you might enjoy:	An environment focused on entrepreneurship. Networking Possibilities: Small-business Owners, Self-employed Contractors, Architects, Consultants

Don't worry if you answered yes to many of the questions. No one will fall completely into one or two categories. As individuals, we're not that easy to define! Instead, view these exercises as a way to discover the environments you enjoy most, and where you'd like to begin networking.

EXERCISE III - THE PHONE BOOK

It's time to get out the Yellow Pages! But don't call people...yet. The Yellow Pages is one of the most valuable networking tools you have in your home. It's a comprehensive list of nearly every company and service in your area, and it's absolutely free! Now that you've clarified your skills, interests and likely work environments in exercises I and II, you can use the phone book to find out where to apply what you've learned.

Take a look at the Yellow Pages Index. The index, although *usually* found in the back of reference books, is at the beginning of the Yellow

Pages; here it lists the categories companies will fall under. Starting with A and ending with Z, go through the index and write down the job categories and titles that appeal to you. For example, if you're an aspiring actor or actress, you might find "Theaters" under the "T" section. Write down your answers in the left-hand "Category" column of the chart below. In the end, depending on how big your phone book is, you should have a list ranging from 5 to 30 categories. Photocopy this chart if you think you'll end up with more than ten categories.

CATEGORY	RANK		
	1	2	3

The next step is to rank the way you feel about each category. Go down the list and put an "x" in the 1 column if the category you wrote down is one you're really interested in. Mark an "x" in the 2 column if it's a category you're somewhat interested in. Mark an "x" in the 3 column if it's a category you're only slightly interested in.

The categories with an "x" in column 1 represent where you should begin your networking journey. Find out what companies in the phone book actually perform the services listed in that category. Write down the names of those companies, and then do a little background research to find out more about them. Before you pick up the phone and dial, read the next chapter to determine exactly what you want to learn from these companies, and whom you want to meet.

other words, don't network without a purpose. Paulette encourages all her clients to know themselves well enough to know who (and what) they're looking for.

YOUR VALUE AND WORTH

No networking experience is ever truly complete until you realize how much value *you* have. Your input is critical, both in your daily environment and in the networking process. Your gifts, talents and interests are important and valuable. You have as much to contribute to networking as the people you're networking with!

During your networking process, you may run into people who try to intimidate you or talk down to you because "you're just a kid." Some might try to squelch your thirst to learn about yourself and the world. The important thing to discover and to remember is: *there's nothing anyone can do to stop you, once you've set a positive course for yourself.* Never let others tell you who you are, where you fit in, or what your interests should be. More than likely, they're wrong.

- Networking is a personal experience as well as a social one. You must assess your skills and interests before you can network effectively.

- Self-discovery is a lifelong process.

- Your true value and worth can never be determined by another person. You must always understand what you have to offer the world, and never lose sight of it.

PICKING THE EXPERT'S BRAIN

Here are some resources to help you learn more:

Tieger, Paul D., and Barbara Barron-Tieger. *Do What You Are: Discover the Perfect Career for You Through the Secrets of Personality Type.* New York: Little Brown & Co., 2001.

Exercises in this book help pair different personality types with relevant careers.

McCarthy, Kevin. *The On-Purpose Person.* Colorado Springs: Navpress, 1992.

This book is designed to help readers discover and accomplish what is most important to them.

CHAPTER 4. Networking With a Purpose

HOPEFULLY chapter 3 has helped you learn more about yourself and where your networking journey might take you. But before you pick up the phone and begin networking, there are some important things you'll need to know.

First, begin thinking of networking as a tool which can be used in many different ways in a number of settings. In order to not misuse the networking tool, you must understand its purpose.

> "It's more important to know where you're going than to get there quickly."
> – Mabel Newcomer

If you needed to nail two pieces of wood together, you probably wouldn't use a screwdriver. When sawing a piece of wood in half, you can't use a roll of duct tape. The same is true of networking.

If you meet with a professional to talk about the kind of work they do, don't spend the whole time talking about yourself and what a great candidate you'd be for an internship. If you meet with a brain surgeon, don't waste their time asking questions which only a heart surgeon would know the answers to. Determine your networking goals before you begin talking with people. Ask yourself what your networking needs are, and then determine who can best answer your questions and offer assistance.

In chapter 2 we discussed the *reasons* for networking. Now, we'll build upon this by discussing the *motivations* for networking. The following paragraphs outline some of the most common motivations behind networking. While reading, please keep in mind that the purpose of networking, always, is to build reciprocal relationships. If you network to get something, like a job, then be up-front about your intention. It's okay to network just to find a job – but be honest about your goals.

Reminder Balloon

Reminder: the purpose of networking is to build reciprocal relationships.

Piece it Together

A reason explains the "why" behind an action. Motivation is the drive it takes to do the action in the first place.

The motivations for networking usually fall into four main categories:

1. To uncover job information: Network to learn more about the kinds of positions that might interest you.

2. To learn about trends: Network to learn about the forces that are shaping the business world today, and to discover how you might fit into the future work world.

3. To meet new people: Network to continue making contacts who you can add to your networking list. Remember, it's a web!

4. To get a job: Network to find the right position in the work world for you.

Let's dive in and look at these four categories more closely. As you read, begin thinking about which category fits best with your networking needs and goals.

UNCOVERING JOB INFORMATION

Are there any jobs that make you think, "Wow! I would really love to do that!"? Are you curious to know more about a job? If so, read on to discover how to network to uncover job information.

What it takes:

Networking is a great way to learn what qualifies a person to work in a certain position. You can learn what different professionals did to land their present job. This will help you decide what type of training and education *you* will need to qualify for a job. For example, corporate lawyers make a lot of money and often work on high-profile court cases. But it takes three years of law school to obtain a law degree – and that's after four years of undergraduate college! Are you prepared to study for seven years *after* finishing high school?

The real world:

There are exciting ways to learn all about different jobs without having to actually perform the jobs themselves. You can follow a professional around for a day in what's called a job shadow, or you can conduct informational interviews which are purely conversational. You can obtain an apprenticeship or internship at a company if jobs there appeal to your interests and fit within your skill set. If you decide that your networking goals involve getting real-life job information, then be sure to read chapter 6 carefully for great details on job shadows, informational interviews, apprenticeships and more.

LEARNING ABOUT TRENDS

It is extremely important to consider the future when doing your job search. You will want to make sure you are not pursuing a career that won't exist in a few years. For example, twenty years ago automotive workers never dreamed they would be replaced by technology. But if you go to an automotive assembly plant today, you'll find that many of the jobs which people used to do are now done by robots. Those in the automotive industry who didn't plan for the future were suddenly and sadly out of a job. Learning about trends that are shaping the work world is as important as learning about the work world itself.

So let's get specific. To network successfully in the "trends" department, you can do the following:

Find out about current and future companies:

What are the leading companies in your area of interest? Which companies are setting trends and changing the way the world does business? For example, have you ever used a computer to write a paper or surf the Web? If so, you've probably been impacted by the computer company, Microsoft™. What other companies are setting trends and changing lives?

Here are some books that will help you learn about companies which are setting trends and changing industries:

► Makra, Kevin. *The Canadian Job Directory.* Toronto: Student Employment Network, 2000.

► Crispin, Gerry, and Mark Mehler. *CareerXroads 2001: The Directory to Job, Resume, and Career Management Sites on the Web.* Kendall Park: MMC Group, 2002.

You can also learn about companies and their development in the following magazines and newspapers:

► *The Wall Street Journal* – A business newspaper in the United States.

► *Forbes* – A magazine for business and investment information.

► *Fortune* – Information on successful companies and the current business climate.

► *Canadian Business* – A Canadian news magazine of business and investment.

► *Report on Business* – A Canadian magazine reporting on the latest in business and investment.

► *Business to Business*
www.business2business.on.ca/welcome.html
– An Internet e-zine focusing on Canadian business issues.

Find solutions to problems:

Ask yourself the following question: What problem was I put on earth to solve? Your mission, should you choose to accept it, is to figure out the *what* and the *how* of this question. The problems don't have to deal with large-scale issues – it can be as simple as creating a solution for your elderly neighbor so they don't have to shovel their sidewalk in the wintertime. Your neighbor may welcome the opportunity to pay you $10 to shovel, just so they don't have to.

As you look at the trends affecting you, your family, your community and your world, begin thinking how these same trends will affect the job you do in the future. Begin networking with experts about the issues they're facing now, *and* the ones they expect to face in the years to come.

Becoming the problem solver you were born to be means becoming an entrepreneur. An entrepreneur is someone who undertakes a challenge to solve a problem. Contrary to what most people think, you don't have to start your own business to be an entrepreneur. The following are some online resources for young entrepreneurs:

► **www.youngbiz.com** – A teenager's guide to networking, careers, investing, business and entrepreneurship.

► **www.yeo.org** – This site is specifically designed for young businesspersons 25 years of age or younger. Chapters exist in both the U.S. and Canada.

► **www.yea.ca** – Support, social networking opportunities and education for young entrepreneurs in Canada; chapters exist in British Columbia, Alberta and Ontario – more chapters will be added in the future.

► **www.realm.net** – The Web site for *Realm Magazine*, a career and entrepreneur magazine for young Canadians.

TO MEET NEW PEOPLE

The best reason to network is for the sake of networking itself. Is there a new teacher at your school? Go up to them, introduce yourself and say hi. Did your favorite restaurant change ownership? Go ahead and meet the new owners. Friends, neighbors, club members and church contacts are a few more worthwhile mentions in the long list of people you can acquaint yourself with. If you think you don't know anyone, the next chapter will help you brainstorm to uncover current and future contacts.

TO GET A JOB

In chapter 1 we mentioned networking to obtain a specific job position. This was referred to as "direct-contact networking." Direct-contact networking means asking, "Can I have a job?" In this case, you will always want to network with the person who says, "You're hired!"

Direct contact is a good road to take if you know you need a part-time or after-school job. Using direct contact, you can network to meet people who might be potential employers. If you're currently in a job that you don't enjoy, or you'd like to find a similar position which pays more, direct-contact networking may be a good route to take. When using direct-contact networking, always be up-front and honest about your reason for asking for your contact's time. If someone agrees to meet with you, don't forget to come prepared. Give your contact helpful information such as a résumé, your work history or a list of references. These will be discussed in more detail in chapter 9.

Direct-contact networking is always most beneficial when used in conjunction with informal networking. For example, if you're using informal networking to investigate jobs that are of interest to you, or problems you're capable of solving, you'll undoubtedly uncover exciting employment opportunities along the way. Informal networking may bring you into direct contact with job opportunities without your ever submitting a résumé or job application.

Now that you know the four motivations for networking, begin thinking about where you fit in. Always ask yourself: *Why am I networking?* It's okay if you can't narrow it down to just one answer; still, try to get as specific as possible, because once you know why you're networking you'll be much more effective at it.

CHAPTER HIGHLIGHTS

- Networking is a tool. It must be used in the right way for the most effective results. Figure out why you're networking before you begin.

  The four motivations for networking are:

  1. To uncover job information

  2. To learn about trends

  3. To meet new people

  4. To get a job

- What problems were you put on this earth to solve? Answering that question will also help you network.

PICKING THE EXPERT'S BRAIN

Here are some resources to help you learn more:

Herman, Roger E. *Signs of the Times: News You Can Use to Drive Your Future.* **Winchester: Oak Hill Press, 1999.**

This book cites trends to watch out for in the future, and how we can use what we see today to guide our actions for tomorrow.

Realm Magazine

This is a quarterly magazine geared towards young Canadians, but the information offered goes beyond the borders of Canada.

CHAPTER 5. You Never Know Who You Know

IN the previous chapters you've learned a little more about yourself and why you're networking. Now it's time for the fun part – brainstorming to discover contacts! You'll be brainstorming about two

"The future is purchased by the present." – *Samuel Johnson*

kinds of contacts: those you know, and those you want to know. This chapter will start by helping you list the contacts you already know, and then we'll build up to brainstorming about the contacts you want to know.

SIX DEGREES OF KEVIN BACON

Have you ever heard of the concept "six degrees of separation"? It's based on the principle that you can link yourself to anyone in the whole world through six other people. For example, you may have a cousin in Germany who knows a banker in Chile who is connected to a lawyer in Scotland.... Within six steps you may be able to connect with someone in virtually any part of the world!

There is another version of "six degrees" called "Six Degrees of Kevin Bacon." It's a game where you try to link any actor or actress with Kevin Bacon in six steps. Here's an example:

Link Kevin Bacon to Tom Cruise in six steps:

1. KEVIN BACON starred with Bill Paxton in *Apollo 13*
2. Bill Paxton starred with Helen Hunt in *Twister*
3. Helen Hunt starred with Kevin Spacey in *Pay it Forward*

45

4.   Kevin Spacey starred with Russell Crowe in *L.A. Confidential*
5.   Russell Crowe starred with Meg Ryan in *Proof of Life*
6.   Meg Ryan starred in *Top Gun* with TOM CRUISE

The good news is that you don't have to be a movie star for the concept of "six degrees" to work in your life! That's because both "six degrees" the game and "six degrees" the principle illustrate the same thing: there are degrees to which we know people and can connect to them.

In this chapter, we're going to use the "degree" concept, but we're going to build off of three degrees instead of six.

For the first degree, you'll be brainstorming to produce the names of those people who are closest to you. The second degree will encompass acquaintances, or people who you don't know very well. The third degree will be brainstorming about people you don't know at all, but whom you would like to know.

Then, we'll go back and figure out if someone in the first two degrees can help you get to a person you want to know in the third degree.

Reminder Balloon

Reminder:
Listing contacts is a good way for you to realize how many people you know. Then you can discover who the people you know, know. Like we said in chapter 1, it's a web!

THE FIRST DEGREE

For the first degree, think of all the people you are closest to. This can include your mom, dad, best friend, etc. The first degree includes the people in your life who you love and depend on, and the people that know you the best. Your first-degree contacts are those people you see on a frequent basis, and with whom you have developed solid relationships.

ILLUSTRATION OF DEGREES

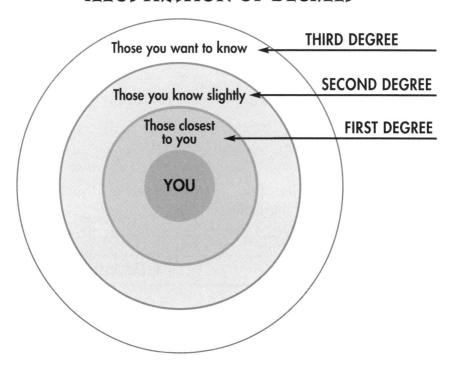

The following bulleted points are suggestions to help you brainstorm. Some of the suggestions might not reflect first-degree relationships for you. You might want to file someone like a coach or neighbor within the category of second degree, depending on your relationship with them. That's okay! Place the names of people where they fit best in your networking world.

- ▶ Parents and siblings
- ▶ Relatives, including grandparents, aunts, uncles and cousins
- ▶ Neighbors
- ▶ Close friends
- ▶ Boyfriend/Girlfriend

- Roommates
- Teachers
- Coaches
- Doctors
- Spiritual leaders (pastor, priest, rabbi, etc.)
- Counselors
- Employers

Make a list of the first-degree people in your life using the table below:

FIRST-DEGREE CONTACTS

NAME	RELATIONSHIP TO YOU

THE SECOND DEGREE

Second-degree contacts are people you know but who you only feel comfortable interacting with in a limited way. For example, at school you might say hi to someone you vaguely know, and then just keep walking. You probably wouldn't stop to talk to this person about your plans for the weekend, or about possibly hanging out together. Other examples might be the waiter at a coffee shop you frequent, or the neighbor down the street that you see sometimes. It can be a coworker you're not too familiar with, a teacher you don't know well, or your best friend's cousin who you met briefly just one time. In all cases, second-degree people are aware of who you are, and you of them. But there's not a close relationship between you.

Before we brainstorm to identify your second-degree contacts, let me emphasize that the goal of networking with these people is not that they become first-degree contacts. Of course, it just may happen that you occasionally form a better relationship with a second-degree contact, but, as a rule, you don't have to develop close relationships with second or third-degree contacts in order to network with them. The secret to networking with second-degree contacts lies in something called *mastering the weak tie*[3], which essentially means becoming skilled at working within casual relationships. In this way, you can know many people without expending the amount of time and energy it takes to maintain all these relationships.

Mastering second-degree relationships is part of your networking journey. Fortunately, there are a number of ways to approach this challenge. For example, take the time to get to know the coffee-shop waiter's name. Send your neighbor a birthday

> **AIN'T IT A FACT**
>
> You don't have to become extra close to second and third-degree contacts in order to network with them. Mastering the weak tie means becoming skilled at working within casual relationships.

[3] Granovetter, Mark, from his 1974 study "Getting a Job" as cited in Malcolm Gladwell's book *The Tipping Point: How Little Things Can Make a Big Difference*. New York: Little Brown & Co., 2000.

card. Congratulate your teacher on the birth of his or her first child. The small things you do to foster a connection with someone can pave networking highways in the future. Little things can make a big difference in your networking success!

Here are some suggestions to help you brainstorm second-degree contacts:

➤ Coworkers
➤ Babysitters
➤ School principals
➤ Friends' parents
➤ Neighbors
➤ Camp counselors
➤ Store owners/workers
➤ Your parents' contacts
➤ Librarians
➤ Community leaders

SECOND-DEGREE CONTACTS

NAME	RELATIONSHIP TO YOU

THE THIRD DEGREE

Are you aware of specific people you want to meet? Are there people you want to know, who could help you make your dreams come true? Did the last chapters help you find people in companies that you're dying to acquaint yourself with? If so, then you're thinking about the third degree of contacts: people you *want* to know.

Just like you did for first and second-degree contacts, you're going to compile a list of third-degree contacts. As you compile this list, keep an open mind. Third-degree contacts can be anyone and everyone. No networking mountain is too high. If you want to network with a public figure such as Madeleine Albright, Bill Gates or Margaret Atwood, then list them! Understand, of course, that it will take a lot of time, energy and effort to connect with these people. You'll also want to go through the right channels and be respectful of their schedules and boundaries. But never underestimate yourself or to whom you can connect.

THIRD-DEGREE CONTACTS

NAME	RELATIONSHIP TO YOU

NETWORKING WITH
THIRD-DEGREE CONTACTS

The big question is: how are you going to network with the people in your third degree? The first step is to review all the people you listed in your first two degrees – you never know who *they* might know!

Begin thinking about the occupations of your first and second-degree contacts. What do they do on a daily basis? Who might this put them in contact with? Think, too, about the organizations they belong to. Are there any clubs they've joined where it might be beneficial to network? Who are their neighbors? Where do they grocery shop? It sounds odd, but people meet others in all sorts of settings. You just never know who you know, and who they know, and who they know, and who they know....

Most importantly, don't hesitate to ask your contacts questions. It's better to be up-front about your quest for networking knowledge than to try to snoop around on your own. Talk to people. Make friends. Ask questions. Be *honest*. If someone is helpful, say thank you, and try to return the favor if possible. Remember, it's all about building relationships!

After all is said and done, you might run into a big fat brick wall. There may be someone in your third degree that you're dying to talk to, but you can't get a foot in the door to speak with them. At this point, all is not lost. You simply have to try connecting with them in a different way. Most likely, this may involve picking up the phone and calling them, or trying to meet with them in person. In essence, you will be asking for an informational interview. This concept will be discussed in the next chapter.

Your search for third-degree contacts should be ongoing. But if you've exhausted your resources for finding them, where do you turn? Where can you get more information? Fear not! The following are some resources that might help you find more contacts:

➤ Walker's Research, LLC. *The Corporate Directory of US Public Companies.* Lafayette: Walkers Research, LLC, 2002.

➤ Canadian Newspaper Services International Limited, ed. *The Blue Book of Canadian Business.* Toronto: Canadian Newspaper Services International Limited, 2001.

➤ Moore, David R. *The Address Directory of Celebrities in Entertainment, Business, Sports & Politics.* Albuquerque: Americana Group Publishing, 1999.

➤ www.hoovers.com – This Internet site will let visitors do keyword searches on any company or industry to obtain information. Press releases on this page often list names of key corporate players.

➤ www.smartdigitaltelevision.com – This page has links to directories and information, including jobs, the Fortune 500 CEO list, the Canadian Yellow Pages and more!

KEEPING TRACK OF THINGS

As you build your database of contacts, it's important to keep track of things. You should always be able to access your contacts easily, and you should know when you last spoke with someone. It's also helpful if you write down what you spoke about, and how you might follow up that conversation.

There are a number of ways you can keep track of things. One way is to write the names of each of your contacts on an index card. You can then file these cards in a way that makes sense to you – perhaps alphabetically, by name or industry. On the front of the index card write the contact's information, including an address and phone number; alternately, you could attach their personal business card to the front of your index card. On the back of the index card, write details about when/if you spoke, left messages, met, e-mailed, etc.

Here's an example:

FRONT	BACK
John Smith, All Together Corporation 330 Hampton Drive Networking City, NY 00110 212-555-3394 johnsmith@networkingtogether.com	10/07/02 Left a message with secretary. Secretary said he'd call back. 10/09/02 Spoke with John. Arranged time to meet. 10/15/02 Met with John personally for an hour. Informational interview. Gave him résumé. John gave me contact name of Ralph Hunter and said to stay in touch. 10/16/02 Followed up meeting with thank-you note.

If you have access to a computer at home, you can use a software program to keep track of things. A computer-generated contact spreadsheet is easy to make, and would include the following categories: Contact Name, Contact Title, Corporation, Address and Phone, Date of Contact, Response (from contact) and Follow-Up. For detailed information on follow-ups, see chapter 9, which discusses the different ways to send a thank-you.

Piece it Together

A database is an organized set of information.

Contacts are persons in your networking web you have – or will have – interaction with.

SUCCESS BY DEGREES

Building your networking base is an ongoing experience. Keep your eyes and ears open for new contacts and new information. Both will come your way often, so be sure to notice!

In all your networking, keep a close friend or relative informed of your endeavors. An informed friend or relative can keep you accountable to your goals, and can encourage you along the way. A second set of eyes might also spot networking opportunities where you don't. Besides, a journey is always more enjoyable when there's company to be shared!

CHAPTER HIGHLIGHTS

- There are degrees to which we know people. First-degree contacts are those in your immediate social circle. Second-degree contacts are people you know, but not very well. Third-degree contacts are the people you *want* to know.

- Great networkers can master the weak tie. That is, they know how to work within casual relationships.

- Use your first and second-degree contacts to network your way to third-degree contacts.

- Keep in mind that if doors don't open that way, you may have to network with third-degree contacts on your own.

- Always keep track of your contacts! Maintain a database with your contacts' information, and a record of when you last spoke.

PICKING THE EXPERT'S BRAIN

Here are some resources to help you learn more:

Shelly, Susan. *Networking for Novices: Making and Using the Connections that Count.* New York: Learning Express Press, 1998.

- Your local **Chamber of Commerce** is a great place to start networking. Chambers of Commerce are filled with – and connected to – leaders, networkers and entrepreneurs.

In the U.S.:

www.chamber.com

E-mail: info@chamber.com

In Canada:

www.chamber.ca

E-mail: info@chamber.ca

• You can also use your local **YMCA** and **YWCA** to meet people and network. They frequently offer mentoring, teaching and community programs that can help you connect with the right individuals. Look in the phone book for the YMCA or YWCA Head Office nearest to you, or visit their Web sites at:

In the U.S.:

www.ymca.net or www.ywca.org

In Canada:

www.ymca.ca/ or www.ywcacanada.ca/

CHAPTER 6. More Ways to Network

THERE are other ways to connect with people and expand the "degrees" to which you network. This chapter will discuss activities that will introduce you to new people, new ideas and new experiences. These are some active ways to do additional networking – to make you captain of your networking ship! Here's a quick look at some of the topics we'll be covering in depth:

"Only the curious will learn and only the resolute will overcome the obstacles to learning." – Eugene S. Wilson

➤ Informational Interviews

➤ Job Shadows and Apprenticeships

➤ Volunteering

➤ Internships

INFORMATIONAL INTERVIEWS

An informational interview is held when you request a conversation to learn about something that interests you. In other words, you will speak with someone, in many cases an expert or a professional, to find out what they know. You can hold an informational interview with anyone, about anything!

The concept of informational interviewing might seem a little strange. After all, you're asking someone to take time out of their busy day to talk to you, and the two of you may be complete strangers! Let me reassure you that informational interviewing is a common practice, and most people will be glad to talk with you. When you ask someone to share in-depth information that they have, you're implying that they're an expert. Most people are flattered by that!

Why do it? Well, not only will informational interviewing give you an opportunity to discover more about the world around you, it also gives you a chance to network with new people. You're building your network by meeting people who do things that you find interesting, and who therefore know things that will be useful to you.

Informational vs. employment

Even if you request an informational interview in a place where you may like to work, an informational interview is not an employment interview. The goal of an informational interview is to obtain information. The goal of an employment interview is to obtain a position.

Piece it Together

The goal of an informational interview is to obtain information.

The goal of an employment interview is to obtain a position.

Where to begin

The exercises and information in chapters 3 and 4 should have given you a good idea of where to find the people you want to talk with. But how do you find a real, live person to talk to? One idea is to pick up the phone.

If you're calling a business, there will usually be a receptionist answering the phones. Tell the receptionist your name, your age and your reason for calling. Most likely, the receptionist will know the right person for you to talk to. She or he can give you a name, and then connect you. If you don't know what to say to the receptionist or are afraid you'll forget, use a script! Here's an example of a script you may use, where you fill in the blanks:

Hello. My name is _____. I am ____ years old, and I would like to learn more about _____. Can you tell me if there's someone in your company who might be able to spend a few minutes on the phone with me, answering some questions?

When you are put through to a contact, always ask them if it's a good time to speak. You may be phoning at a busy time, and you don't want to be an inconvenience.

Here's an important tip: An informational interview can be informal, but it shouldn't be unstructured. When you get ahold of a contact, do not assume the receptionist informed them of who you are, or of your reason for calling; tell the contact why you're calling and provide a bit of information about yourself. Have a rough sketch outlined of what you would like to talk about.

What to Ask

What you will talk about during your informational interview will be determined, for the most part, by what you want to know. If you find yourself stumped without any questions to ask your new contact, here are a few suggestions:

- What do you like most about what you do?
- What do you dislike the most?
- Where can I get more information about _____?
- What do you recommend for someone like me who is interested in _____?
- Is there anyone else I could speak to about this topic, to whom you might refer me?

Things to keep in mind

Many people are hesitant to initiate an informational interview because they fear that asking for information will make them look stupid. If you have these feelings, let me assure you that informational interviewing does not make you look stupid, it makes you look smart. *Here's why:* you are taking the time to uncover information about a subject you would like to know more about, as well as meeting people who may be beneficial connections; that makes you appear very professional. You are researching and evaluating your interests, your contacts and your future – this puts you head and shoulders above many of your peers! Most people you talk to will immediately realize you're doing something that only a few exceptional youths ever attempt. They will be predisposed to help you *because* you're helping yourself. People who understand the value of what you're attempting will certainly understand the value of *you*, too!

JOB SHADOWING

One way to learn what a job is really like is through job shadowing. The term job shadowing refers to following a professional around for a day to gather information about the ins and outs of a specific position. Job shadows can vary in length from an hour or two to the whole day. It's up to you and your host to determine what structure best fits with you both. Job shadowing is a part of networking in which you get to learn what a job is really like – and not just what the want ads say!

How to set up job shadowing

Your school guidance counselor should have information on job shadowing, and he or she can help you find a career that's a good match with your skills and interests. Your parents and the contacts in your first and second degrees can also help you with job shadowing. They may know someone to call if you already have a field of interest picked out.

JOB SHADOWING

Apprenticeships are an in-depth version of job shadowing. An apprentice is defined as a person learning a trade by working in that trade for a specific period of time. In other words, apprentices learn by doing. Apprenticeships require a high level of commitment, and you must be 16 years of age or older to participate in a Department of Labor sponsored apprenticeship program in the United States. Here are some resources if you are interested in pursuing an apprenticeship:

In the U.S.:

➤ Oakes, E.H., ed. *Ferguson's Guide to Apprenticeship Programs.* Chicago: Ferguson Publishing, 1998.
Look for this apprenticeship guide at your local library. It will give you an overview of programs available to you, and provides application information as well.

► *Office of Apprenticeship Training, Employer and Labor Services*
Web site: www.doleta.gov/atels_bat/
See this Web site for apprenticeship eligibility and requirements, finding a program, information by state and more!

In Canada, apprenticeship programs are available through provincial government offices. To find out what each province and territory offers, check out the following Web sites:

► **Newfoundland and Labrador:**
www.gov.nf.ca/youth/post/app.htm

► **Nova Scotia:** www.ednet.ns.ca/training.html

► **New Brunswick:**
www.gnb.ca/ted-fde/apprenticeship/index.htm

► **Prince Edward Island:** www.apprenticeship.pe.ca/

► **Quebec:** www.emploiquebec.net/anglais/qualif/index.htm

► **Ontario:** www.edu.gov.on.ca/eng/training/training.html

► **Manitoba:** www.gov.mb.ca/educate/apprent

► **Saskatchewan:** www.sasknetwork.ca/pages/et/et_128.htm

► **Alberta:** www.tradesecrets.org

► **British Columbia:** www.itac.gov.bc.ca

► **Yukon Territory:**
www.gov.yk.ca/depts/education/advanceded/apprenticeship/index.html

► **Northwest Territories:**
http://siksik.learnnet.nt.ca/04%20apprenticeship/index.html

► **Nunavut:** Although there is currently no Web site specifically for apprenticeships in Nunavut, the Department of Education is the ministry responsible for these programs.
See their Web site at: www.gov.nu.ca/education.htm

VOLUNTEERING

Volunteering is defined as the willing undertaking of a task, usually with the outcome of assisting another person. Motives for volunteering may vary, but the best reason for wanting to volunteer is a desire to serve others. The benefits flow from there. One benefit is that you get to meet a variety of people and can potentially network with them. But don't let networking be your *only* motivation for volunteering. To truly be a successful volunteer, you must have an aspiration to accomplish a goal while united in a common cause with others.

Where do I start?

There are some important questions you will want to ask yourself before you run out and join the Peace Corps. Consider the following:

► **What are you passionate about?**
It's best to volunteer at an organization you believe in. If you're against deforestation, don't volunteer for a lumberjack committee. If you love to wear fur, don't volunteer for PETA (People for the Ethical Treatment of Animals.) Find a place where expression of your values and beliefs is encouraged, and where you feel like you can make a difference.

► **What do you want to learn?**
Volunteering means the giving of your time to benefit a cause or organization. But benefits can also be a two-way street. Try to determine, before you volunteer, what you would like to learn from the experience. Is there certain information you want to obtain? Are there certain experiences you wish to have? What, about this experience, might help you down the road? When you investigate a volunteer organization, talk to the agency's Director of Volunteers. Ask them if they, or someone else within the organization, will assist you with your goals.

► **How much time can you commit to volunteering?**
It's important to talk over all volunteering decisions with your parents or guardians. Work with them to determine a schedule that accommodates everyone as best as possible. If you're under 16 or don't have a car, your parent or guardian may be driving you to and from your volunteering position, so it's important that you know their schedules before you commit to anything. Also, take into consideration how much time you need for homework, socializing, or after-school activities. All these things take time, and you need to make room for them. The last thing you want is to be burned out after your first day of volunteering!

Finding a volunteer organization

If you've determined your goals for volunteering, you can begin talking to people about possible opportunities. First, seek out contacts within your first and second degrees. Is there anyone who might share your interests and want to volunteer with you? A parent, teacher or guidance counselor will probably have a good idea of locations and organizations that might be a good fit for you.

The Internet has lots of resources for finding volunteer organizations. Check out the following:

► *Action Without Borders* (International): www.idealist.org
A site to post and find volunteer opportunities.

► *Amigos de las Américas* (International): www.amigoslink.org
Amigos sponsors volunteers between the ages of 16-25 in public health and environmental projects in Central and South America.

► *Charity Village* (Canada): www.charityvillage.com
This is a site for Canadian-registered charities and Canadian public service agencies to post their need for volunteers.

► *Volunteer Canada* (Canada): www.volunteer.ca
More Canadian volunteer opportunities.

➤ **SHiNE (U.S. and Canada):** www.shine.com
An online database of volunteer opportunities.

➤ **SERVEnet (U.S.):** www.servenet.org
A U.S. site to post international volunteer opportunities and interests.

➤ **Volunteer Solutions (U.S.):** www.volunteersolutions.org
This site will match you with a volunteer organization using your home state and your area of interest.

Reminder Balloon

Targeted networking has the specific purpose of locating a job or transforming a career.

Informal networking is ongoing, everywhere, in a variety of settings.

Volunteering will create opportunities for camaraderie and exchange with others, thereby lending itself naturally to networking. Remember, volunteering provides a great opportunity to use *informal* networking, but is not the appropriate place for *targeted* networking.

CASE IN POINT

Erik Karulf is a freshman at Eden Prairie High School in Eden Prairie, Minnesota. Erik uncovered his love for technology at the age of 3. He taught himself everything he could about computers, and eventually started to pass along his knowledge by helping others, beginning in the second grade. Erik continued to tutor and assist throughout middle school and into high school. "My goal was to show myself [as being] helpful and friendly. I gradually built up a reputation for myself as the 'request fairy' when it came to solving computer problems. When teachers and students had computer issues, they came to me."

Eventually Erik's reputation as a computer whiz reached the ears of the technology coordinator at Eden Prairie High, Dianne Myers. Dianne and Erik pooled together to form a group consisting of technology-savvy students, which they named Tech Cadre. Tech Cadre works with teachers, network administrators and students to make sure all the technology at the high school is running efficiently. Erik's work here has led to other opportunities as well. "The drama teacher at school had a computer problem, and I helped out. I have a love for drama, especially in lights and sound, and I wanted to get some hands-on experience in that area. So I offered to help out with the drama Web site. That led to more opportunities where I could use my technology skills to help out with drama productions."

Erik's opportunities and connections were the result of his willingness to reach out and help others. "Volunteering is a lifestyle," says Erik. "Some great opportunities have come my way because people know I'm helpful, and I can be counted on. Volunteering has opened numerous doors in my life."

INTERNSHIPS

Many successful people have started their careers working as interns. Did you know Bill Clinton was an intern? He learned about politics and the ins and outs of Washington by working as an intern under Senator William Fulbright.

What is an intern?

According to Dictionary.com, an intern is a student or a recent graduate undergoing supervised practical training. Interns usually work in a structured setting such as an office, agency or bureau.

The role of interns varies immensely, depending on which organization you intern with. During my own senior year of college I did an internship at a magazine out of Boston called *Cultural Survival Quarterly*. Certainly I had my share of dull tasks on the job, such as writing letters or fetching bagels from across the street. But I also got to research and write two articles which were published in the magazine. Good internships will always balance the good with the bad. Internships should present you with unique opportunities to learn and to develop specific skills which will make up for the times you may have to do some serious 'grunt' work.

What to expect

You can expect to meet a number of diverse people while you intern. From bosses to secretaries to maybe even the President, internships can expose you to faces and places that might otherwise go untapped in your networking endeavors. In addition to developing skills for the future and gaining experience, you'll encounter people that can help you fulfill your goals and dreams.

Now for the more realistic side of things: internships usually involve a minimum time commitment during the week, which is up to you and your employer to determine. Some summer internships might be full-time, while others might range from five to 20 hours per week during the school year. Just as commitment levels can vary in internships, so can other factors such as pay. Some internships will offer financial reimbursement for your time, while others will require you to work for free. Depending on the internship program you choose, you may get academic credit. Talk to your parents, guardians or guidance counselor to determine if you can receive academic credit for your internship.

Internship information

The following resources will have more information on internships:

▶ **Oldman, Mark, and Samer Hamadeh.** *America's Top Internships.* **New York: Princeton Review, 1999.**
This book discusses internships within the United States, in fields like law, environment, journalism, modeling and much more.

▶ **Green, Marianne Ehrlich. Internship Success:** *Real-World, Step-by-Step Advice on Getting the Most Out of Internships.* **New York: McGraw Hill, 1998.**
A user-friendly guide for obtaining the internship that suits you most.

▶ **Donovan, Craig, and Jim Garnett.** *Internships for Dummies.* **New York: John Wiley & Sons, 2001.**
This book is in the "Dummy" series, and is full of internship information.

▶ **www.work4teens.com** This is a career resource Web site for U.S. students between the ages of 14 and 23. This site even features a successful internship provider each month.

▶ **www.youth.gc.ca** A career-planning and internship Web site for youth in Canada.

- Informational interviews, job shadows, volunteering and internships represent opportunities to meet new people, gain experience and develop skills.

- Informational interviews are not job interviews. The goal of an informational interview is to simply obtain – you guessed it! – information.

- Job shadowing means following an individual for a day to find out what a job or company is like, without having to work there.

- Volunteering is a lifestyle. Before your volunteer, make sure to determine your interests and passions, what your goals in volunteering are and how much time you can commit.

- Internships are opportunities to gain real-world job experience while meeting new people in the process.

PICKING THE EXPERT'S BRAIN

Here are some resources to help you learn more:

Greene, Rebecca. *The Teenagers' Guide to School Outside the Box.* **Minneapolis: Free Spirit Publishing, 2001.**

This book provides information about alternative learning experiences including internships, job shadows, mentoring and more.

Landes, Michael. *The Back Door Guide to Short-Term Job Adventures: Internships, Extraordinary Experiences, Seasonal Jobs, Volunteering, Work Abroad.* **Berkeley: Ten Speed Press, 2001.**

1,000 easy-to-read listings for short-term, off-the-beaten-path, work-and-learn adventures.

CHAPTER 7. Breaking the Fear Barrier

FOR all its benefits, networking certainly can be a frightening activity. After all, it's daunting to call up strangers on the phone or to meet with them in person, no matter how strong your motivation for doing so may be. It's even harder to try to build relationships with networking contacts that you've only just met. Networking is such an over-whelming activity for some people that they never even try it. Fear can keep you in the same social and professional spheres forever.

"You gain strength, courage and confidence by every experience in which you really have to stop and look fear in the face. You must do the thing you think you cannot do."
– Eleanor Roosevelt

The good news is, if you're slightly introverted or if you find meeting new people difficult, there is still a ton of networking potential inside of you. This chapter is devoted to activities and information which will help you overcome fear barriers and continue on your networking journey.

COURAGE ISN'T THE ABSENCE OF FEAR

Fear is not a bad thing to feel. It's a natural emotion which is vital in certain situations. If you're in the woods and are suddenly approached by a bear, fear is necessary. Otherwise, you might stick around and try to make friends with a wild animal instead of running away – not a very smart choice!

Fear only becomes harmful when it prevents us from taking on new opportunities for growth and development. While it's not a bad thing to feel fear, it's a bad thing if you let it control your life.

WHAT SCARES YOU THE MOST?

Will Rogers once said that even if you're on the right track, if you just sit there, you'll get run over. Since you are reading this book, it's clear you are on the right track in life or are trying to get there; now it's time to make sure you keep moving.

To make progress, it's important to identify potential obstacles in networking. One of the biggest obstacles you can encounter is fear, so you must ask yourself: *What scares me the most about networking?* Is it calling someone on the phone whom you've never met? Is it a fear of sounding stupid? Is it that you're afraid you'll meet someone and they won't like you? How about the thought of being at a professional lunch and accidentally dropping food all over the front of your shirt?

No matter what the root of your fear is, your feelings are legitimate. There is no stupid reason for feeling fear – it's what you choose to do with that feeling that matters.

THE ID EXERCISE

The following exercise will help you identify and deal with your networking fears. For the first part of the exercise, list the things about networking which scare you the most. In the second part of the exercise, you will prepare yourself for a scenario in which some of your fears come true. Here's one example from my own life:

Part One: Identify the root of the fear

I am scared of attending my first Chamber of Commerce meeting, because I don't want to be the left-out new person. I fear cliques, and that no one will talk to me.

Part Two: Prepare for that scenario

I imagine attending a Chamber of Commerce meeting where everyone is giving me the cold shoulder. No one is remotely interested in me. I'm silent, talking to no one. This is very discouraging. So what should I do? I try to find someone near my age and initiate a conversation with them. I get the focus off me by asking them tons of questions about themselves. (Note: people love to talk about themselves.) My solution is to be the initiator and not wait for others to talk to me.

Okay, so there's an example of fear from my life. Believe me, there are others. There are many things about networking which scare me – and I'm the one writing the book! Even the most seasoned networkers sometimes feel fear, so don't worry if you do, too. Take a moment to think of four or five things that really scare you about networking, and then think of some creative ways to prepare yourself for overcoming specific scenarios.

CASE IN POINT

Prasantha Jayakody of Seattle, Washington, knew a friend of a friend who had experience starting companies. As a young entrepreneur, Prasantha wanted to talk to the contact and learn all he could. "That's where things stopped for a while," explains Prasantha. "I was reluctant to talk to him, because I thought all my questions would sound stupid. I didn't want anyone remotely well-connected to think badly of me."

Eventually, Prasantha decided that the benefits of networking with his contact outweighed the potential harm. "I knew that the process of starting a company relies greatly on networking, and I figured it would be easier to overcome the fear now, rather than when the company could be directly affected."

Prasantha phoned the contact, who agreed to meet. Before the meeting, Prasantha did strategic research so that during the meeting he could stick to specific issues. "[This person] was really receptive," says Prasantha, "especially because I came prepared and didn't waste his time. Part of overcoming my networking fear was just [summoning] up the courage to pick up the phone. The other part of overcoming my fear was doing my homework and being prepared."

THE THREE Pʃ

Another way we can avoid feeling nervous or scared in networking situations is by initiating what I call the three Ps – prepare, practice and pull yourself together! By doing your best to accomplish each of the Ps, you'll have a good chance at overcoming obstacles and eliminating fear when you network.

Prepare

To prepare means to make or get ready; the act of preparing may take many forms. For example, if there's someone you want to call on the phone, prepare for the phone call. First, draft a telephone script like the one in the last chapter. Know in advance what you want to say. Prepare yourself in case you reach a receptionist who says some tough things like: "The person you want to speak with doesn't take unsolicited phone calls," or "Why should I put you through?" If you prepare yourself for the worst-case scenario, then you'll be ready for anything.

You can prepare for face-to-face meetings in the same way as well. If you're meeting with someone about an interest you have in their job or company, find out as much as you can about them *before* you go into the meeting. Visit their Web site if they have one, and research the company itself; see chapter 4 in this book for ways to uncover more information about companies you're interested in.

Practice

Practice what you want to say over and over. When you're sure about what you want to say, you will feel more confident about saying it. That confidence will extend to your voice, and people will be able to hear it. Smile when you talk on the phone, because friendliness is audible. By the same token, nervousness and fear can be heard over the phone, too. Concentrate on speaking in a clear, level voice and keep your breathing as even as possible. Remember to take deep breaths before you dial, and calm yourself down as much as possible. The more calm and collected you are, the calmer the person on the other end of the line will be, too.

You can prepare for one-on-one meetings by practicing your questions or even by conducting a mock interview. Sit down with a parent or friend and ask them to role play with you; they could pretend to be the person you're meeting with, and you could practice asking questions and talking with them.

Pull yourself together

Have you ever had a "bad hair day"? Have you ever been in a situation where your clothes got ripped or stained and you still had to wear them? I've had both those scenarios happen – and trust me, it was no fun!

Part of the reason these experiences are so frustrating is because most of us feel confident when we know we look our best. Putting your best foot forward regarding your appearance can give your confidence a boost. Here are a couple of things to remember when preparing to meet face-to-face with a networking contact:

➤ **Good grooming isn't just for poodles:** Remember to do those day-to-day essentials – bathe, brush your teeth, comb your hair and put on deodorant. Your chances of networking successfully are greatly improved with good hygiene.

➤ **Find out what they're wearing – then go one step up:**
What you'll wear when networking will depend a lot on who you're networking with, and where. If you're networking with your Uncle Bob at the family barbecue, shorts and sandals are the dress code of the day. However, if you are meeting with someone new in a professional setting like an office, the rule of thumb to follow is to find out what the office dress code is, and then go one step up. For example, if you're meeting with the president of Lawnmowers, Inc. and everyone at the company wears jeans and T-shirts to work, you'll want to go one step up, so maybe you'll wear khakis and a nice shirt. If you're meeting with the CEO of a large company where the employees wear suits all day, it's hard to go one step up unless you don a tux or a formal gown. Since that's not really appropriate, just wear a suit, too. Business suits for both men and women are the most formal thing you can wear to the workplace.

▶ **Bring along the essentials:** The right outfit is only half the battle in pulling yourself together. Don't forget to bring accessories like a pen, paper, or a résumé (if you have one). Even if you're not interviewing for a job, you still want to bring these things along. Your networking contact might say something you really want to remember, so you'll be glad you've got something to write it down with. They might want to know more about you, and a résumé is a good way to show what skills, talents and experiences you have. It also shows that you thought about the meeting beforehand and did your best to come prepared.

Piece it Together

A fashion accessory is an extra item of dress.

A networking accessory is an extra item, such as a résumé, which facilitates networking relationships.

A FRIEND INDEED

Another way to overcome your networking fears is by being accountable to someone. Accountability means that you answer to someone for your actions. To be accountable in your networking process, draft some goals and show these to a close friend. This friend has permission down the road to ask you how it's going and to make sure you're doing what you said you would do. Ideally, accountability works because a friend won't just bug you about networking – hopefully they'll encourage you, too.

You and a friend may also want to take a networking journey together. If you both begin networking at the same time, then you can share similar experiences with each other. The expression "safety in numbers" definitely applies here. You and a friend can go to different functions together and network, which may seem less scary than going alone.

JUST DO IT

Even with a group of friends, networking might still be scary. Different personalities react differently to meeting new people, and that's okay. If networking scares you to death, keep in mind it's not the number of strands that count in your networking web, but rather the quality of the individual strands. Work strategically to find a few contacts who you're comfortable speaking with, and with whom you can develop good relationships.

Reminder Balloon

Networking is not about accumulating as many contacts as possible – it's about connecting strategically with quality individuals.

CHAPTER HIGHLIGHTS

- Fear isn't a bad thing to feel. It's a natural emotion which is vital in certain situations. Fear only becomes harmful if you let it control your life. One exercise that can help you overcome networking fears is to:
    1) Identify some of your networking fears
    2) Work out positive solutions for exact scenarios

- Put the three Ps to work in your networking endeavors: prepare, practice and pull yourself together!

- Include other people in your networking journey. Choose a friend, and either be accountable to this person about your networking goals, or begin networking at the same time as them and share your experiences along the way.

PICKING THE
EXPERT'S BRAIN

Here are some resources to help you learn more:

Palmer, Pat, and Melissa Alberti Froehner. *Teen Esteem: A Self-Direction Manual for Young Adults.* **Atascadero: Impact Publishers, 2000.**

This book helps teens build skills and attitudes to meet today's real-life challenges.

Carlson, Richard, Ph.D. *Don't Sweat the Small Stuff For Teens.* **New York: Hyperion Books, 2000.**

100 suggestions on dealing with everything from stress to bad hair. This book uses stories to encourage you to be all you can.

CHAPTER 8. Recognition and Respect

CEOs, company presidents, millionaires, famous celebrities, writers and local heroes are a few examples of the people you might meet when networking. On your way to net-working with these high-level professionals, chances are you'll run into their *support staff.* Support staff includes administrative assistants, receptionists and service personnel; these people are the backbone of the work world, ensuring that the day-to-day functions of an office or a particular work environment run smoothly. Whether it's through answering phones, scheduling meetings, paying bills or running the office in a number of ways, these people are an essential part of any successful business. Chapter 8 is devoted to explaining the crucial role support staff plays in net-working, and to making sure that all support staff get the respect and fair treatment they deserve.

> "Give to every other human being every right that you claim yourself."
> – Robert G. Ingersoll

A BAD RAP

Sadly, some people think that workers in support-staff positions are annoyances blocking access to the person they *really* need to talk to, usually someone higher up in the chain of command. As a result, support-staff members are overlooked and disre-garded or, in the worst cases, treated disrespectfully. While I'm sure that everyone reading this book treats others with the utmost courtesy and respect at all times, this chapter may help improve the way service positions are perceived.

When networking, it is important to handle *all* support-staff contact appropriately. The categories below show two different approaches to support staff. Category 1 reflects a poor attitude toward support staff, whereas category 2 reflects a positive outlook about support staff. When networking, make sure that all your thoughts, or at least behaviors, line up with the second category. If you have beliefs that show you fall into the first category, read on to uncover some steps you can take to change your outlook and your behavior.

The motivation for treating everyone with courtesy *should be* that you would wish to always be treated with courtesy yourself. Remember, too, that the labels people wear in the office are not their only labels in life; they're also cousins, brothers, mothers, friends and neighbors. They deserve respect no matter what role they're playing. Choose your words carefully when speaking to support staff. You never know who you're talking to, or who might be around the corner listening.

Category 1

Support-staff personnel are annoying people who hinder contact with the "higher-ups" in a company.

Networking is only worthwhile when done with key power players. No one else is worth the time or effort.

It's not important to treat support staff courteously. They are just the lowest rungs on the business totem pole.

Category 2

Members of a support staff, like all other people, deserve kindness and respect.

Support staff should not be used as steppingstones to reach someone higher up in a company or position.

Individuals on a support staff can be the key to unlocking doors of possibility. They may have power and influence beyond their job description.

As you can see, categories 1 and 2 convey very different attitudes! The attitudes expressed in category 2 are held by people who truly want to succeed at networking. This is because successful networkers realize that anyone and everyone is worth talking to, regardless of position or job title. Successful networkers treat all people the same, regardless of rank. The attitudes in category 1 convey that someone's rank or status determines how they should be treated. This is a poor way to network and an erroneous view of people in general.

INFORMATION AND UNDERSTANDING

Understanding what support-staff personnel actually do on a daily basis can help us to better appreciate them, and will thus help us to show them respect. While the support staff performs a number of different activities depending on the organization or the employer, we as networkers will usually interact with them in only a handful of ways.

Members of the support staff are usually the first people we run into when we're contacting an individual or company for the first time. In this capacity, the support staff may include security guards, secretaries, receptionists, personal assistants, etc. When we encounter support staff during our attempt at initial contact with their boss or company, their goal is two-fold. First, they want to ensure their supervisors' or coworkers' physical safety; second, they want to protect their supervisors' and coworkers' time. Ultimately, the support staff wants to make sure you have a legitimate reason for taking up the space and time of the person or people they work for.

When you first encounter support staff – whether in person or on the phone – there are a few rules you can follow so that they know how to handle your networking requests.

➤ Identify who you are, using both your first and last name.

➤ Explain your purpose for calling (or showing up) as specifically as possible.

➤ If you have a meeting that's already been set up, let them know immediately.

➤ Set a time limit and stick to it. Tell them how long your visit will be.

➤ Don't be offended if they need to verify the information you've just given them. Try to look at things from their perspective; *you're* the stranger.

➤ Be prepared to show identification. Don't leave home without it!

Piece it Together

Recognition is the act of acknowledging and/or validating someone.

Respect means showing esteem or consideration toward another person.

APPEARANCES CAN BE DECEIVING

As just noted in category 2, members of a support staff can unlock doors of possibility. This is because status, titles and appearances can be deceiving. In many cases, the support staff has the ability to aid you greatly. Overlooking support staff, or worse, treating them poorly, means overlooking potential opportunities. During my second job out of college, I witnessed this principle firsthand.

Angie was the name of the receptionist at a company I once worked for. She was a bright, energetic, dynamic woman who held the office together like glue. Part of Angie's job was to greet people as they came through the front door. Most of the people Angie interacted with were as friendly with her as she was them. They enjoyed her warmth and personality. But there were a few who simply treated her as "just the secretary." In fact, there were a handful of job candidates who disrespectfully snubbed Angie while waiting for an interview.

What these job candidates didn't realize was how highly the general manager regarded Angie and her opinion. After the interviews, the general manager would linger at Angie's desk and ask her what she thought of the job candidates. A candidate who had been disrespectful to Angie was hardly ever considered. The reasoning was that if they treated Angie poorly, they might do the same with a client. This would reflect badly on the company, and could also mean a loss of business.

A positive or negative word from Angie could mean all the difference when it came to hiring someone at that particular company. Support staff may have the same effect on your abilities to network successfully, depending on how you treat them. Here are some general rules to follow to show support staff courtesy and respect:

► **Ask a support-staff person his/her name when you meet. Make the introduction as warm as possible.**

► **If you have a business card or résumé, hand these out to the support staff just as you would the higher-ups in the company. Ask if they have a business card you can take in return.**

► **If support-staff personnel offer you a beverage, don't ask for a high-maintenance drink (e.g. iced tea with lemon). Ask for "anything hot" or "anything cold." In this way, you'll be showing respect for their time, as they probably have better things to do than to fix you something to drink.**

WORKING YOUR WAY UP

When dealing with support staff, keep in mind that you may be in their shoes one day. Even with a college education, support-staff roles in entry-level positions are perfect for new graduates. In addition, internships (as discussed in chapter 6) are essentially support-staff positions. Although interns will likely have the opportunity to learn other skills, an internship definitely has its share of support-related tasks such as photocopying, making coffee, answering phones and handling people!

CASE IN POINT

It was a cold, bitter day when Sheldon Hunt arrived for work. He sat at his desk with a sweater on to keep the chill away. Soon, an older gentleman entered the office; his hair was uncombed, his coat disheveled, and he carried a stack of papers clamped under his arm. The frumpy-looking stranger received only terse looks from the workers at the front of the office. No one would greet him, much less ask him what he needed. Curious, Sheldon got up from his desk and approached the stranger. For all appearances, Sheldon judged him as a tired, older salesman working well beyond his intended retirement age.

After a short chat, Sheldon found out this man was an investor in the company. He was wealthy and well-connected, and was visiting the company to provide them with a handful of well-placed and well-qualified sales leads.

Later, this unexpected giant gave Sheldon a key to the future. He told Sheldon to check out a new company that he was partially funding. They were creating some cutting-edge products that were right up Sheldon's alley. Sheldon later went to work for this new company, where he received a significant increase in benefits and salary.

"This guy was recognized as being one of the most well-connected, respected business investors in the local community," says Sheldon. "If I had ignored him like everyone else, I would have missed out on some big opportunities."

KEEPING IT REAL

Human, face-to-face interaction is necessary to learn what the work world, like any new environment, is really like. There is a point at which library books, the World Wide Web and the newspaper cease to be helpful. Contact and conversation with other human beings is critical to successful networking. Knowing this, we must always show the people we meet while networking our utmost respect. This is true of everyone we encounter, not just applicable to the people we want to network with the most. Support-staff members are critical in making the work world and the entire world function properly. They, like all people, deserve admiration and respect regardless of rank.

CHAPTER HIGHLIGHTS

- Support staff aid in the day-to-day functions of an office or a particular work environment.

- Support-staff members, like all people, deserve kindness, consideration and respect.

- A support-staff person often has the ability to help and assist networkers in powerful ways. Don't overlook their potential!

- You, too, may be in a support-staff position one day. These roles are perfect for new college graduates in entry-level positions!

PICKING THE EXPERT'S BRAIN

Here are some resources to help you learn more:

Lewis, Barbara A. *The Kid's Guide to Service Projects: 500 Service Ideas for Young People Who Want to Make a Difference.* Minneapolis: Free Spirit Publishing, 1995.

Lewis, Barbara A. *What Do You Stand For? A Kid's Guide to Building Character.* Minneapolis: Free Spirit Publishing, 1997.

CHAPTER 9. Next Steps

DIFFERENT tools are at your disposal along the networking journey. Depending on where you're at in the networking process, the tools you need may vary. These tools can include

> "The toughest thing about success is that you've got to keep on being a success." – *Irving Berlin*

résumés, business cards, cover letters and thank-you notes. This chapter discusses, in detail, some of these additional resources you may want to consider when networking.

RÉSUMÉS

This book has previously mentioned the word *résumé* a few times. You may be wondering, "What is a résumé, anyhow?"

A résumé is a document which highlights your job experiences, education and specific qualifications for a position. It is text which is designed to tell an employer or professional more about you. Résumés can vary in length, depending on age and experience. When you are starting out, it will be one page. For someone who has been in the work force for many years, it may be longer. Regardless of length, résumés should be clear and succinct. Employers are busy – the more concise and to the point, the better.

A résumé is often referred to as a "silent salesperson" – that is, it will emphasize your professional qualities without speaking a word. The accomplishments outlined on your résumé will be of interest to many people you network with!

The primary use of a résumé is to obtain a job interview. But in networking, résumés are useful in other ways, too. For example, I recently conducted an informational interview with a professional speechwriter to learn more about the world of speechwriting, which is something I've been interested in lately. At the end of the informational interview, I gave this speechwriter my résumé. I wasn't trying to get a job as a speechwriter right then; rather, I was giving them a document that told them a little bit more about me, my education and my experience. It was a gesture of courtesy. The next time I contact that person, they can take a look at my résumé as a refresher, to remind them who I am.

Reminder Balloon

An informational interview is a conversation with someone to learn about a topic that interests you.

When creating your résumé, here are some general rules to follow:

➤ Keep it simple. Create clear, concise sentences with bold section headings such as: Education; Qualifications; Work Experience; etc. Keep it to one page *unless absolutely necessary* that you add more.

➤ Use power words and phrases. Instead of saying, "Worked on the sales floor," say something with a punch like, "Assisted customers and coordinated merchandise handling."

➤ Your résumé should be error-free, so have a friend or family member check it over for mistakes once you've finished it.

➤ Make it attractive. Use high quality paper in a conservative color like white, cream or gray.

What your résumé will look like and say will depend largely on whomever you're submitting it to. For that reason, there are different formats résumés can take. For an example of a résumé, see the sample included at the end of this chapter. Some other good examples of résumé formats can also be found at the following Web site:
www.jobweb.com/resources/library

Scroll down and select the link: <u>Interviews & Resumes</u>. On the next page, select the bullet point that says <u>More Sample Resumes</u>.

This Web site is also a great resource for general career information for young people. It's primarily designed for college students, but don't let that stop you from scrolling through. You will find articles on employment trends, and tips on various experiences like interviewing and even job fair information. If not now, this site may be very useful to you in a couple of years!

COVER LETTERS

If you're submitting a résumé to obtain a job, it should be accompanied by something called a cover letter. A cover letter is a one-page letter addressed to the potential employer. It can be broken down into four parts:

1.   Make sure the employer has easy access to your contact information; your name, mailing address, phone number and e-mail address should all be at the top of the cover letter for quick reference. Don't forget to also include the employer's title and address, as well as the date! Remember, it's a formal letter.

For a sample cover letter, see the link:
www.content.monster.com/resume/samples/coverletters/letter2/

2.   The first paragraph of the cover letter should include a short introduction of yourself, how you learned about the job opening, and your objective in submitting a résumé.

3.   Next, spark the employer's interest in you. Highlight any specific skills and qualifications you can bring to the position. For example, if you're submitting a résumé to be considered for a position as a florist and you have experience arranging bouquets, be sure to mention that in the cover letter.

4.   Finally, in the third paragraph, express your interest in the job and ask for an interview. Some thing like, "I would like to meet with you to discuss this position in further detail" always works nicely. Be sure to mention that your résumé is enclosed.

As with all letters, yours should be addressed to someone specific. Never send a cover letter with the line, "Dear Sir/Madam" at the top. If a specific name is not easily accessible, call the company you're applying to and ask for the name, title and address of the person in charge of hiring for your position. Finally, make sure all names are spelled correctly and that your letter is error-free.

Piece it Together

A résumé is a one-page document highlighting your job experience, education and specific qualifications for a position.

A cover letter is a one-page letter accompanying a résumé on its way to a potential employer.

THANK-YOU LETTERS

When you've had the good fortune of networking with someone, be sure to follow up the conversation or meeting with a thank-you note. Whether you're thanking your contact for the opportunity of a job shadow, an informational interview, a job interview or anything related, send a note expressing your gratitude for their time and attention. Make the letter as specific as possible by mentioning topics you discussed or additional contacts you met. Here are some things to remember when writing thank-you letters:

➤ Send the thank you out the day following your meeting or conversation. The sooner you write it, the less time you will spend worrying about remembering to send it!

➤ A thank you can be typed on a sheet of paper or written on a card. If you choose to write your thank you on a card, pick a simple or traditional design that will not distract from your message.

➤ If the conversation was informal and/or conducted solely on the phone, you may send your thank you via e-mail, if it is more convenient for you. If you decide to use e-mail, make sure it comes directly from you. Refrain from using a third party like BlueMountain.com to send complex graphics and singing messages.

BUSINESS CARDS

When networking, it is sometimes important to have a quick means of identifying yourself to a new contact. That's what business cards are for. Business cards are a way of passing along your pertinent information to contacts without taking up much of their time.

You may be thinking, "What would I put on my business cards?" Even if you lack a snappy job title, don't let that stop you from creating the perfect business card. All you need on the card is your immediate information: name; address; phone number; e-mail. Anything after that is extra and not absolutely necessary.

In the past, cost has prohibited many young people from creating business cards. But now, general competition among retailers and the advent of the Internet has driven prices downward. In fact, there is a Web site where you can get business cards for free! Check out www.vistaprint.com. This site has business card templates you can choose from – then you fill in your personal information on the card. VistaPrint will print your cards for free, and the only cost you absorb is the shipping. If you choose standard ground mail, you pay about $5.00 for 250 cards.

READY, SET, NETWORK!

This chapter has listed some additional networking tools. With the exception of thank-you notes, these tools are not necessary for successful networking. They are simply additional steps you can take to further your networking experience. There's no reason to wait until you have a sparkling résumé and snappy business cards before getting out there and talking to people. In fact, that wouldn't match up with our definition of net-working, which is building mutually beneficial rela-tionships. Résumés, cover letters and business cards are not critical supplies in relationship-building – they're icing on the net-working cake.

AIN'T IT A FACT

Résumés, cover letters and business cards are helpful when networking, but not absolutely necessary. Keep in mind you can still network even if all these tools aren't in place.

- A résumé is a one-page document highlighting your job experiences, education and specific qualifications for a position.

- A cover letter, included with a résumé when applying for a particular job, is a one-page letter addressed to a potential employer. It brings the most basic and important information about you to the employer's attention.

- Always send out thank-you letters after networking with a contact. Make your thank you as specific as possible by mentioning topics you discussed or additional contacts you met.

PICKING THE EXPERT'S BRAIN

Here are some resources to help you learn more:

http://www.e-teen.net/index.htm

This site offers a variety of teen-related resources. Check out the career-planning section, which has résumé, job hunting and interviewing information.

Ireland, Susan. *The Complete Idiot's Guide to Cool Jobs for Teens*. New York: Alpha Books, 2001.

This book is full of information related to writing résumés, cover letters and interviewing. As you already know, working can be a great way to network!

SAMPLE RÉSUMÉ

Lara Zielin
500 South Street
Minneapolis, MN 55422
612-555-8997 (home phone) 612-555-5412 (cell phone)
E-mail: lara@larasresume.com

OBJECTIVE: Obtain a sales position in the field of publishing

EDUCATION: B.A., Parker College, White Bear, MN. Honors: Cum Laude
Major: Anthropology
Additional Courses of Study: History, English Literature, Biology

EXPERIENCE: Marketing Communications Specialist
Fortune Marketing Corporation, March 1998 to Present
• Maintain client relations and communications with international and domestic resellers
• Target reseller markets and assist in closing of sales
• Plan and execute annual tradeshows, including follow-up and sales lead development
• Coordinate design and production of all print and electronic advertising, including redesigning promotional and marketing materials

News Writer
Minnesota College News Bureau, September 1997 – March 1998
• Developed story ideas and wrote press releases, news articles and public relations material
• Produced news in conjunction with KBBR radio, The Minnesota College newspaper and the Office of College Relations
• Communicated with local and national television, radio, newspaper and magazine reporters

Copywriting Intern
Publishing Everything Magazine, November – December 1997
• Assisted with copy editing and layout
• Researched current events pertaining to publishing
• Wrote two articles accepted for publication in the magazine

SKILLS: Windows, Access, PowerPoint, Word, Excel, Adobe Photoshop, Quark

VOLUNTEER: Habitat for Humanity
Spanish tutor

CHAPTER 10. Networking for a Lifetime

THE goal of this book has been to outline ways to successfully network with others while setting career goals and learning about the "real world." In this final chapter, you'll be exposed to additional principles surrounding networking that will keep you connecting with others long after you've turned the last page of this book. More than just an activity, networking can be a state of mind, an attitude and a lifestyle.

> "We are prone to judge success by the index of our salaries or the size of our automobiles, rather than by the quality of our service and our relationship to humanity."
> – Martin Luther King, Jr.

NETWORKING = LEADERSHIP

Establishing genuine relationships is not just part of networking – it's a part of leadership. All successful leaders care about the needs of others, and successful networkers will do the same. The best networkers will always be the ones asking what they can give to the relationship as well as receive from it.

In his book *The 21 Indispensable Qualities of a Leader*, author John C. Maxwell writes about essential leadership traits. The leadership guidelines that he outlines are also important in networking. Here are a few of Mr. Maxwell's rules that I feel are among the most important to network by:

▶ Never focus on rank or position – focus on the person.

▶ Be aware of others' needs. Ask, "How can I help?"

▶ Achievement, fame and recognition are never as important as treating people correctly.

BE THE CONNECTION

Networking is as much about finding connections as it is about *being* a connection. While you search out contacts, look for ways you can *be* a contact for others also seeking connections. When looking for people who can offer advice, assistance or information, try to be aware of people for whom you can provide the same.

Are you one of too many people who think that you don't have anything to offer? Think again.

> "I teach in order to learn."
> – Robert Frost

There are always ways to help others – it just may not be the same way others are helping you. For example, while many of your contacts may be helping you to find a job or by answering questions, you can help someone who just needs a friend. *Big Brothers Big Sisters of America* is just one organization devoted to connecting mentors with children who need support during their early years. To find out more about being a friend to a child in need in the United States, check out the *Big Brothers Big Sisters of America* Web site: www.bbbsa.org

In Canada, you can visit the Web site for *Big Brothers Big Sisters of Canada* at: www.bbsc.ca/

These programs are among many available. Review chapter 6 for more details on volunteering and on *becoming* a connection.

Keeping your chin up

When *you're* the connection, and *you're* the one people are turning to in their networking endeavors, you'll have many reasons to be thanked. You'll be providing a service that is priceless. When you are helping others in such a valuable way, it's natural you'll want to be thanked, whether verbally, through a note in the mail, or with a handshake and a smile. Most of the people you provide networking assistance to will express their thanks accordingly. Yet sadly there will be those you help who do not say thank you; there will be some who accept your knowledge, experience and advice, and then wander off without a word. It can be hard to have a good attitude in the wake of such negativity. To keep yourself from becoming bitter or discouraged, focus on the benefits of helping others instead of on the drawbacks. Sometimes it's best to simply give, expecting nothing in return. If you can do this, you will always know that you did the right thing, even if the other person did not. Continue to thank others as you'd want to be thanked, and express gratitude just as you'd like to receive it.

STEP BY STEP

Don't despair if, right now, your contact list is only five names long. As stated in chapter 1, networking is a lifelong journey, so your contact list may take some time to grow.

Don't worry; there are things you can do today to make the most of your current contacts:

Referrals

To refer is to send or direct someone to an authority or source of information. When you network, you can ask a contact for a *referral* – to *refer* you to someone with additional information or contacts that you don't currently have. For example, in one networking instance I heard about, a networker interested in a medical career spoke with a brain surgeon about this profession, but the networker didn't get all of his questions answered. In fact, during the conversation the networker became interested in the anesthesiologist's role. At the end of the discussion the networker politely asked the surgeon, "Is there someone else you recommend I speak with? Perhaps you can refer me to an anesthesiologist?"

Recommendations

A recommendation is a favorable report, made about you, which is given to a third person. A good recommendation can be used to open difficult networking doors. Using the example from above, let's say that our networker was having a hard time getting ahold of the anesthesiologist. The networker might then go back to the brain surgeon and ask to be *recommended* to the anesthesiologist. The surgeon then asks the anesthesiologist, in one way or another, to make time for the networker.

Recommendations come in many shapes and sizes. Some are very informal and casual, like the recommendation that would pass between the surgeon and anesthesiologist in this scenario. Some recommendations are more formal, like the kind needed to help get an acceptance into a university. Formal recommendations usually consist of a letter, written to a school or potential employer on your behalf, by a teacher, mentor or former employer. Some recommendations are made via the phone – like the time one of my well-connected contacts telephoned an important political figure and asked, on my behalf, that this person squeeze a meeting with me into their busy schedule. With most recommendations that you require, *you* will have to take the initiative and coordinate the type of recommendation you want or need.

Piece it Together ←

A referral is the process of moving from your current contact to an alternate authority or source of information.

A recommendation is a favorable report made about you to another person.

BAMBOO

Even with referrals and recommendations, beginning to network is a lot like bamboo.

Bamboo is a highly versatile and adaptable plant, found at locations ranging from sea level to 13,000 feet in altitude. Like most plants, bamboo initially sprouts and grows from the earth. Unlike many other plants, however, bamboo takes a while getting started. Bamboo stalks can remain at the same height for long periods of time. Some stalks may grow only an inch or two a year – year after year. But finally, once the bamboo plant has grown deep roots and has firmly established itself, it shoots up like a rocket! It can grow inches upon inches in a single day!

Just like bamboo growth, networking takes time and energy, and nearly everyone starts from the same place – ground level. Networkers slowly build their contact lists and meet new people at the pace which best suits them. Inch by inch, name by name, the contact list grows. Your contact list will be no different – until one day you'll need a name or a phone number and you'll already have it! Or you'll find yourself in the right place at the right time. Best of all, you'll lead a more fulfilling life because you endeavored to learn all you could while making connections that count.

Networking can have a dramatic, positive effect on your life. Constantly strive to meet new people, ask questions when you're curious, and enjoy the different directions you take during your life's journey. Make a connection, *be* a connection, and benefit from these enriching experiences. This life is yours to lead, and yours to shape – keep a smile on your face, and keep your eyes open for ways to make things happen!

- Establishing genuine relationships is not just part of networking – it's a part of leadership. The best networkers will always be the ones asking what they can give to the relationship, as well as receive from it.

- Networking is as much about finding connections as it is about *being* a connection. When looking for people who can offer advice, assistance or information, try finding people for whom you can provide the same.

- Referrals and recommendations can be used to further your contact list. Use the connections you have now to expand your networking web.

- Networking is a lot like bamboo. It might take a while to get started, but once firmly established, it can take off!

PICKING THE EXPERT'S BRAIN

www.madeforsuccess.com

Chris Widener has put together a Web page dedicated to helping readers make their lives more meaningful and productive. Sign up for the weekly e-mail newsletter!

www.larazielin.com

This Web site offers additional information about networking and about *Make Things Happen*. If you have questions, you can e-mail me, the author, at: lara@larazielin.com

Your comments are also welcome. I look forward to hearing from you!

GLOSSARY

Accountability With relation to networking, accountability refers to keeping someone else current on your networking activity.

Apprenticeship A specific period of time in which one learns a trade by working in it.

Connectors Networkers who can maintain casual relationships with large numbers of people.

Contacts Individuals who make up your networking web.

Cover Letter A one-page letter to a potential employer addressing interest in, and qualifications for, a specific position.

Database An organized set of information.

Direct Contact Networking with the specific purpose of seeking out people who hire for job positions.

Dress Code The standard of apparel worn within a particular environment, in this case, a professional environment.

Employment Interview An interview with the goal of obtaining a job position.

Entrepreneur Someone who undertakes a challenge to solve a problem.

Expert One who is knowledgeable or skillful in a specific area.

First-Degree Contacts Individuals in your networking sphere to whom you are the closest.

Informational Interview A conversation with someone, held to learn about a topic of interest.

Interest A curiosity, focus, hobby or concern.

Internship A period of supervised training undergone by a student or recent graduate.

Job Shadow The act of following a professional around for a day to learn about a specific profession.

Job Title A career label indicating status and responsibility.

Mentor An experienced and trusted guide.

Motivation The drive to do an action.

Networking Accessory Any item, such as a résumé or business card, which facilitates networking relationships.

Occupation An individual's job or profession.

Qualification Competency for a specific task, usually a job.

Reason The "why" behind an action.

Recognition The act of acknowledging or validating someone.

Recommendation A favorable report made about an individual to a third party.

Refer The act of sending or directing someone to an alternate authority or source of information.

Respect Esteem and consideration which is shown toward another person.

Résumé A one-page document highlighting job experience, education and specific qualifications for a position.

Script Pre-written text to help networkers conduct informational interviews.

Second-Degree Contacts Individuals in a networking sphere who are known, though not intimately.

Skill An aptitude or expertise.

Structured Setting An environment which has been prepared for effective networking through research and forethought.

Support Staff Persons who aid in the day-to-day functions of an office or workplace.

Targeted Networking Networking to find a job or change careers.

Third-Degree Contacts Individuals who you do not know, but who you would like to meet and include in your networking sphere.

Vocation A person's employment, trade or profession.

Volunteering Willingly undertaking a task, without pay, usually with the goal of helping another person.

Weak Tie An acquaintance or casual social connection.